THE 2024
ONE PAGE POETRY
Anthology

ONE PAGE POETRY

EDITED BY COLIN GRAHAM

One Page Poetry/The 2024 One Page Poetry Anthology

www.onepagepoetry.com

Printed in the United States of America

The 2024 One Page Poetry Anthology/ One Page Poetry -- 1st ed.

ISBN 9798346099529 Print Edition

All proceeds from the sale of this book will go to the World Wildlife Fund and Oceana, two organizations dedicated to the protection of endangered species and the preservation of their natural habitats.

In celebration of the beautiful art of poetry

Publisher's Note

Out of respect for the amazing poets who have contributed to this anthology, the individual poems have not been edited in any way and fully represent the original presentation of each poet. In some cases, poems required formatting to fit the size restrictions of the book and the ebook, but in no way did this formatting change the original wording or grammatical presentation. Since the individual poets represented in this anthology continue to own the copyright to their poems, the poems are not exclusive to this publication, and we encourage the poets to distribute their work as widely as they choose.

A SPECIAL THANKS
TO OUR 2024 JUDGES

monique jonath is a twenty-two-year-old queer black poet from Oakland, CA (the ancestral lands of the Ohlone people) and a recent graduate from Brown University, where they studied gender and sexuality studies and psychology. They started writing poetry as a joke in early high school, but it quickly became one of their biggest passions. They were a finalist for the position of Oakland Youth Poet Laureate in both 2018 and 2019 and their work has been published in the Youth Speaks anthology Between My Body and the Air (2020), Visitant Lit, and in the Sixteen Rivers Press youth poetry contest. They were also a finalist and a winner of the writer-voted Sixfold poetry contest. In their free time, they are a peer sexual health educator, contemporary and African dancer, and music enthusiast.

Mark Graham is a critically acclaimed novelist and poet who has been writing professionally since 1988. He has written and published five critically acclaimed novels: *The Harbinger* (Henry Holt & Co.), The *Missing Sixth* (Harcourt, Brace, & Jovanovich), *The Fire Theft* (Viking Penguin), *The Natanz Directive* (St. Martin's Press), and *The Five Portals* (Castle Knight Press). He has also written two acclaimed collections of poetry, *Parents Are Diamonds – Children Are Pearls.* (Amur Books) and *And Wrap Your Arms Around Living* (Castle Knight Press).

Ann Tinkham is a published author, ghostwriter, and editor based in Boulder, Colorado. Her fiction and essays have appeared in Apt, Blood and Bourbon, Denver Syntax, Foliate Oak, Slow Trains, Synchronized Chaos, The Adirondack Review, The Citron Review, The Literary Review, Toasted Cheese, Wild Violet, Word Riot, and others. Ann's essay, "The Tree of Hearts" was nominated for a Pushcart Prize and her story, "Afraid of the Rain" was nominated for Sundress's Best of the Net Anthology. She's the author of *Climbing Mountains in Stilettos* and two story collections, *The Era of Lanterns* and *Bells and Stories I Can't Show My Mother.*

Mridvi Khetan, MK, is a budding Indian writer, currently pursuing a double major in Psychology and Economics as well as a minor in creative writing at the University of Chicago. She placed first in the One Page Poetry competition in 2022 and received an honourable mention in the 2023 contest. Her work has been previously featured on Delhi Poetry Slam, publications on campus and her own personal writing blog. She has also been a semi finalist in the honourable Cultural Weekly's Jack Grapes Poetry Prize 2020. MK is also passionate about slam poetry and often performs in her hometown Delhi, India.

Bridge Over a Bone River
Lollie Butler, Tucson, AZ

In a border town built on drought and tourista dollars,
I walk through stalls of silver and tequilla
while along la frontera,
two men and a woman lie flat, handcuffed.
   One will not live to be deported.

Crossing this "bridge over a bone river,"
each became a Christo, carrying the cross of his own body.
In the end, God became a tree, a lizard, or a cloud.

When the sun over Sonora hammers,
every living thing is pummeled down into the earth
where it waits for nightfall to rise and howl.

This is a siesta town, but it is where my country north of here
sleeps. Under our eyes, the nameless dead collect.

We will awaken when a 'migra's rifle fires,
or when the ghost of compassion returns to ask
what we've done with our inheritance.

One wears a ragged shirt, the other a baseball cap,
and the woman wears a crucifix around her neck.
   I might forget them
had I not seen their faces as I drive north toward home,
   silver bangles cold against my wrists.

Instead of Visiting You in the Memory Center
Chelsea Kerwin, Baltimore, Md

I vacuumed, watered the plants, grocery shopped,
worked weekends for time and a half pay. I walked
the dog until he started limping, took him to two vets,
purchased him an orthopedic bed with oversized bolsters.
No one used the word degenerative, but the cabinets
filled with pain pills and peanut butter. I moved in with
the man I want to spend my life with, he taught me
how to use his record player, how the needle recreates
the song by soaring over deviations etched in the vinyl.
We people-watched at the festival, I bought a flower crown,
the mead and Shakespeare made the world spin.
I read a book full of rotting snow and frozen-shut eyes,
outside a blizzard, inside Ares staring out the window.
I decorated the townhouse with gnomes and fairy lights,
travelled to Italy, got engaged on a cliffside in Sorrento,
ranked wedding venues all over Maryland. We drove out
to Massapequa for grandma's funeral, I made a speech
in your place. I told everyone over and over you were ok,
you were comfortable, happy. Her death couldn't touch you.
I stayed with mom after her surgery, took out her trash,
washed her hair in the kitchen sink, filled her birdfeeder.
I made a photo album of our last family trip to Alaska.
In my favorite, a small figure snaps a picture of a mountain.
I put a broken record back in its sleeve. I kissed my good
boy goodbye between two farewell shots at the final vet.
I smoked pot and watched black and white movies,
I searched the basement for mold and mildew, cried

and journaled and didn't even bother railing at God.
I slept in and made love to my fiancée. On karaoke night
I sang Sister Golden Hair and Love is a Rose. I ate mushrooms
and visited you astrally. You were alright without me. Why not?
Didn't I live as you taught me? If guiltily, if sometimes low,
I still caught the occasional sunset, stepped out into several
warm weather rainstorms, I cooked crispy skin chicken thighs
and danced like a jackass in the kitchen to our favorite songs.

I tell the ocean
Hayden Park, Irvine, CA

"I tell my piano the things I used to tell you." –Frédéric Chopin

I tell the ocean the things I used to tell you, these
lulling waves that wash my soul clean of the
worries that always whisper at my knees, my
fingers, the parts of my body that go untouched,
and I'll make do with the sand, instead of your touch
that I craved so much. Sitting on the rocks like
some expired sunrise, today, I'll tell the ocean
everything I used to tell you yesterday, all the things
I missed so much. I hope those crashing waves
will remind me of all that old bitter pessimism, like
kites on the horizon, so wonderfully far away, so far
even if I close my eyes I'll never see them again.

I tell my violin the things I used to tell you. While
playing the melancholy lines, I leaned in, and,
sotto voce, my bow told me to sever the ties that held me
like a vice to your heart. The melodies lilted like the
morning, and I realized I'd been waiting for something
that would have burnt me like cold ashes biting ice
over long-cremated hope. When my violin speaks to me,
I realize it's my own voice, echoing inside all this
ancient wood. The Plowden del Gesù was made from
old-world tonewood, and now I breathe in that old
Cremonian air, the faint pencil tracings, measurements
like a tailor around my breast. Your touch is like this
one, with its secrets held in the intense varnish, and
I wonder how your arms will feel around my waist.

I'll tell you the things I used to keep to myself. I
will be the first by your bedside, reciting stories
that are more than fiction. In our memories, we lived
so vividly and laughed like there was everything to
live for. I want to jump off this waterfall with you
and slide down because that silent rain can. I
wonder if it's just the drizzle collecting on the
sidewalk, dappling like a forest floor, or tears,
like the drizzle on your face falling from windows
I left open. I didn't rush to close them this time,
not wanting to miss that cool mist through the screen
on my cheek. And I wanted to hear the sky bleed
to remind me even heaven has wounds like mine.

They Say She Suffers From Depression
Amy Gordon, Gill, MA

Mother is a storm-bent tree
on the edge of a bluff, her trunk stunted,
shorn of leaves—she twists and twists
against a background of fluffy clouds.
     Fluffy is a childish word.
Mother, says the child, you can have my wings.
I know they are childish, but I am a child,
you can take my wings.
     Wings aren't practical.
The child colors in the herd of clouds.
Violet. Dark blue. A scratch of black.
Mother is a storm-bent tree.
     Who painted these clouds?
     They are supposed to be white.
The child walks to the river.
Have you heard of the great bird
in the Arabian Tales, the one
who hunts elephants, whose wings
cast a giant shadow over hills and plains?
The child finds the bird's egg, smooth and round.
     Leave the rock outside.
Mother, says the child, do you see
the cardinal's nest outside my window?
     I can't see,
     the sun is too bright.
Take my eyes, says the child.
Take my eyes and see with them.

They are childish eyes, but I am a child.
See the blue sky, the green leaves, the red bird.

That is not art.
The child reaches inside her chest.
Here, Mother, says the child. Take this.
Take my heart.

I couldn't possibly. My allergies . . .
The child lies in bed and sings.
The child lies in bed and pretends
to play the banjo.
The child lies in bed and pretends
Mother is a storm-bent tree and in the tree
is a nest, and the child pretends
she lives in the nest.

Monarchy
Avery Kline, Hamburg, NY

Robes of silk crafted from aching hands

A glimmering headpiece, each jewel catching the light we never could quite bask in

The ribbons tied around her waist swish with each step she takes, floating like the limbs of

jellyfish, suspended in the depths of the blue below,

the tide rushing over your feet.

You're a lot like the tide, you know?

She is too.

Something so real yet so fantastical at once.

You exist and yet you are so great that one cannot help but question if the brilliance before their

eyes is but a product of the hour of sleep they lack.

You both rush in and out of our lives, so brazen and bubbly, each word you say like a bullet to

the chest, flowers blooming in my ribcage, my bones startled by your praise.

I've never felt this way before.

Neither have you, it seems.

Oh, neither has she.

Masked poise, forced mirth. All of it hiding the tears in her beautiful ruined bodice.

You were never quite as great, but to me, you were everything.

Your bruised knuckles trace over her skirt, combing through each of its intricate layers, searching

for a sheet that had yet to be ripped.

I tried to tell you. I really did.

You never listened. You dropped the garment and left, never to return again.

I cannot blame you for that. You were hurting.

I was too.

So tell me, why is it that her headpiece had lain broken for so long, her silk dress torn, her

brocade corsets mutilated by the stresses of court, unfixed all the while?

She still stands there now, that smile plastered across her face. You watch her in envy.

I can't help but wince at the sight.

You never knew your place. She had known hers since birth. So why is it that I feel she still

walks in aimless circles, searching along the coast for those jellyfish ribbons in absolute silence?

You wonder why my own hands are bruised, my smile fallen.

But all that matters now is that her dress is fixed, each hem perfectly sewn.

Celeste (My daughter, stillborn)
Lollie Butler, Tucson, AZ

Through the window, the sky stares me down.
With a sleeve, I rub my breath away.

You left as though you'd forgotten your coat or mittens.
       My child,
you are a native of light, blinding to us.

Each night, I tuck a small transparency
under my pillow
and dream the child you might have been.

It tilts my smiles, turns every goodbye on its end.

How I reckoned with God, the giant beekeeper,
to be his drone, carrying my honey home.

Were you transplanted, like a pink radish
to more fertile loam?

Filled with expectation, I hummed
like the rock-a-bye mother I was to become
    and felt a listening inside;
tiny ear cocked against the concertina of my lungs.

My grandmother's body, barely eighteen,
released its early hold.
Three small graves snuggle in beside hers.

The little christening gown
passed through the family hangs empty again.

Tiny traveler, you shine where the blossom
never becomes fruit. What's left goes to seed;
　　white crib in a white room,
doll with stunned eyes leaning against the window.

What is grief but a longing to reclaim;
　　　to hold with fierce resolve all that is dear to us.

At dusk, scanning the sky for new stars,
　　　　I give the brightest one your name.

There is me, apart
Ava Keck, Auburn, CA

There is my day
With shaking hands and nodding heads and deadlines and objectives
    And then there is you
The moon
With your gelato scooped craters
And magnanimous concurrence with us
There is my alarm, blaring obnoxiously
Followed by keyboard clicking and report making and email corresponding
    And then there is you
The waves
Inhaling your vanilla satin foam towards your reflection in the sky
Before collapsing upon your sculpted stones
And then heaving upon yourself, wobbling in seeming amusement
"Again!" says your splash, as you, afresh, gleefully jump at the sun
There is my inbox, pinging
of itemized expenses and budgetary conservatism
    And then there is you
The wind and the trees
Dancing as one, your rhythm bouncing the spotlight from the olive
fronds to the coarse red bark
To the blue bird awakening to the music, to soon sing along
    And then there is me
Inside
What are you doing, living thing? Come join in our revelry!
I sigh out my sentience
Primly, and forcefully:
I'm sorry, dear friends, for I have bills to pay

Friendship
Tempe Javitz, Menlo Park, CA

A golden bond twix bough and leaves,
Summer's sunshine united these.
A clouded hilltop, a steel blue sky,
Who's to say what's hill, what's sky?
The blue green grass along cemented walks
Knows no boundary, grows up through rock.
Thus, it is with friends, you and I.
We blend, mix, grow and tie
An unseen knot that never dies.

The Night Before
Bella Wright, Mead, CO

My Senior year
My last in their home

And as I try to soak up the scent
I realize
My childhood teddy bear no longer smells like my own

We sold the old house not so long ago
But I still couldn't tell you which used to be my tree
I can't explain the way the old porch was concrete
And it didn't creak
I think

And my little brother doesn't need my help anymore
And my sister is taller by inches and more
The cups must have creeped closer to the floor
Because tonight I realized
I have no one left to reach them for

I didn't grow up
I became someone's daughter
It must be something in the water
That makes me slowly fade away
A ghost made of clay
I beg
Sculpt me into a person you will still need someday

I wonder when the time will come for me to slip out the screen door
And let it slam behind before
I sink into the paved floor
Beg the concrete to keep me
In heaven
Back when I was seven
But I leapt off the asphalt when it burned my little feet
And started a game I will never beat

Calendars and clocks rip me from the earth instead
If they are nice they let me keep my roots in exchange for my head
And let me look back as they swing me away
To tell my little sister again that I wish I could stay
Even if I don't
I don't tell her it's hereditary
Change keeps me from rotting
It's only necessary

But I let myself be sad tonight
Because you would think with all this insight
I could hold the key

But my childhood teddy bear still no longer smells like me

Breathe in to larapuna
Lily Davidson, Fitzroy, Australia

she wonders might i rest my eyes
know the place try the inhale
of home's colours
then –

what is the colour of salt?

azure – perhaps cornsilk

but how is the colour of space?

bone

what of exhaling waves? simple

blue violet – blue yonder – blizzard – carolina – celeste

what is the shade of sun that tricks tepid?

flirt – flame

yet burns for days?

atomic tangerine

what is the falling tide to leave the hills of sand, then?

black coral – cultured pearl

and what is the colour of mother hooded plover, nimbly tending her nest low
in wind trodden wildflower?   *fawn – fern – fallow – field – flax*

and our skin goosebumped?

baby powder

the colour of squinting to horizon – to know a buoy a pod a ship a rock
hope a whale?

saffron – dark sea green

what is the colour of the smell of smoke lingering from old fires?

brown sugar – burnt butter – burnished – umber

how could there be words for the gradience of gums?

all the musk bud slates never emulate the stories in those branch knots my dear colour of parents ahead, held hands / our pup once dancing through legs

coffee and cream – cinnamon – cherry and apricot –

and copper and brass – amber – to violet – to lavender

– to love

breathe in to larapuna

hold till lungs burn

brick red

leave the sludge / city

charcoal

exhale wave released ashore

drawn out once more

to larapuna

breathe home.

Pass the salt
Danielle Tomkins, Berkhamsted, United Kingdom

"I LOVE you" never felt like *pass the salt*
It always felt like bubbles up my spine.

You were THAT song I'd play
Over and over again.

My name felt safe in your mouth,
You were mesmerizing.

I would wake up shaking with childlike excitement
If I knew my day had you in it.

You derailed my ordinary and led me to my edges.
The view from us was breath taking.

My favourite sentences started with we,
My favourite me started with you.

Do you remember the time we stayed awake
Talking all night to stall sunrise?

Do you remember the time when hearing
THAT song didn't burn our eyes.

Do you remember the time you made me cry and said it wouldn't
happen again...

Do you remember the time you made me cry and said it wouldn't happen again...

Do you remember the time you made me cry and said it wouldn't happen again....

Your words aren't curly anymore,
They are sharp and they bite me.

Your I LOVE you's
Now feel like salt in my wounds.

I wake up shaking
If my day has you in it.

My name is too good for your mouth,
You are terrifying.

My worst sentences start with we,
The worst you now starts with me.

So I have to let you go now
Before my eyes adjust to the dark.

Does God Write Haikus or Free Verse Poems?
OlaRose Ndubuisi, Pittsford, New York

Life is a poem.

It does not go on forever.
It is limited by
The constraints of syllables, a vocabulary so minimal,
A rhyming scheme, an indescribable dream,
The Author's thoughts of death, and the Subject's will to live.

The throne has grown soft
From the pressure of idleness.

Muscles have grown stiff
From trying to (de)compose
A body of work

Without a skeleton.

How can a poem,
So sentient and alive,
Yet an idea

That humans contrive,
Differentiate between a word
Of repentance and a word of resentment?

How can a poem, no more than words combined,
Compare the sun to a jewel,
Without awaking for school each day
To experience the anaphora it conveys?

It is selective
Like an angel at the gates of Heaven,
While allowing emotions to flood in
Like a remorseful sinner's confession.

Not every word that exists is there,
But every word that is there exists
Because of the words that aren't.
A poem persists.

Twenty One
Loretta Rose, Kansas City, MO

"If you could keep your 21 year old body for the rest of your life, do you think you would?"

You asked me this in the car, playful in tone as a shield to mask the projection of your fears
But I've watched you analyze decay
And pray there's black magic in the mirror

I foreshadowed the ripples in my skin deepening
With every birthday wish blown
My palm a maze of barb wire
Like cross stitch poorly sewn
And from the carvings in my face
Time would never be hired
To sculpt the foreheads of LA
To paint New York when she gets tired

But to be shackled with youth is a vow I'll never swear in
Because this body's womb is a desert, barren
Too young to know to listen when the wise owl hoots patience
It yearns for sun when the crops get their rain in

The days melt to years
And my body, a log
Engulfed by life's fire
Slowly it is gone
No fountain of youth or hyperbolical marketing

Could erase the stains of my skin's markings
Rust spots found on my shoulder and thighs
Or the cracks by my eyes enhanced each time I cry

I'll always want you to love me
Like my 21st year inside of this body
Until the light in the room somehow gets closer
I inhale knowing, now it is over
Returning into earth
I am the ground, I am the dirt
I become the crops that thirst for rain
I become the owl, I know patience's name

Interrupting your monologue, I pierce the air with a sigh
I could never keep this body
That's as old as the universe, for matter doesn't die
I am infinite, a collection of moments in time

(You Believe) Faith
George Harvilla, Dumont, New Jersey

elevated your entreaties to the Creator,
granted you the open parking space.

That afternoon in the library sub-basement,
Osmanthus (the cardigan-self-camouflaged
and oddly-named prayer group moderator)
bemoaned her struggle with perennials
– her astilbe, juncus, hellebore, salvia –
and, obliquely, she accepted remedies
(*try finer mulch or ground eggshells*),
advice from the retired Staff Sergeant
(generally quiet, as war shapes men),
the white words beneath his blazer:
6 tours in Afghanistan and all I got
was this lousy T-shirt... and PTSD.

Not funny, you say.

You don't know how funny,
he winks with one pale eye.

Across town, a mother
clutches her daughter's hand.
They are 28 and 4, respectively;
Shaeron and Faith, respectively;
mournful & resigned, respectively.
One holds her own blood in her arms,

the other's own blood rages against
her own small body with low white
cell count & metastases, respectively.

These are the songs of our world:
perennials & the war-weary
struggle hard to reach light
and you pray for a parking spot
as a mother prays break walls
to hold back Faith's cancer.

Know your audience, the Creator says.
Your melody's predictable;
the lyrics, at times, too hollow.
Rewrite. Then sing it for me, again.

Aberdeen
Erica Gray, Austin, TX

I did not know seagulls
lived in Scotland.

20 years and thought
they were made on the shores
of Lake Michigan
to pick the abalone-bones
of whitefish
and their cataract eyes.

Do seagulls sleep?
It seems to me they were always there.
Rising with the sun.
Raising the alarm.
Marking time with a lover.
Or another.

Do you remember the day he disappeared?
Laid fallow in a field
with mud-soaked knees
and daffodils
the color of his hair.

I would have stayed
in that single bed forever.
I did not know.

I've never learned to like the sea.
46 years
and her dark belly churning
still feels like the end.
Her short-tempered waves
beat the drum
as the clouds bear silent witness.
And the seagulls cry
in great revolt.

If Flowers Wrote the Bible
Ariel Fabrega, Paradise Valley, AZ

Said Sun to Earth: "I pray you hear this plea.
Yoke my rays to your richest soil and forge
what hitherto we've missed. That like a tree,
yet not a tree, bound by light, compelled
to stretch between us to heaven." And up,
from humble sprout and hidden root, sprang
in joyful glory: the first sunflower.

Childhood Hauntings
KaTrina Jackson, Olathe, KS

I think we're all a bit haunted
by ghosts of childhood dreams—
of friends and places long forgotten,
of shadows and shades that gleam.

A brand-new toy that got misplaced,
a date you couldn't face,
a recipe you can't quite remember,
but that you can almost taste.

A place that you can almost name,
a voice you can't quite hear;
the golden glow of summer days,
the serenity of silent tears.

Memories fade and dim with time,
but the spirits still claim our souls.
I think part of adulthood,
is letting our childhoods go.

St. Dunstan Standing
Kate Bullock, New York, NY

Where the light passes through,
you might think me broken,
marred by the enemy of love.
You might think me, too,
a shell of my former self.
Do not do me the disservice of
seeing only my destruction.
Look closer at the afternoon light
kissing the overgrown ivy.
Watch the birds weave and sing,
too free to be confined by stone.
When the wind whistles
and you hear the song of yore,
hear my joys and my cries
to hold them both in equal measure.
I stand here before you now,
decimated and whole.
No worse for what was
but fortified by what remains.

They knew my secret
James Shaw, Corpus Christi, TX

before i ever knew—the lie of things—
the way that planets turned—i wondered why
my friends had chores to do while i wandered

through fields that summer burned—beneath the sun
i scaled the wooded hills beyond those fields
to gain Olympic heights—and in a park

where stones skipped rills for thrills—i scavenged all
the treasures within sight—old coke bottles—
tin cans crusted with rust—cigarette butts

below—homes were so small that i could hide
them with thumbs—while i'd just make-believe friends—
i never played with dolls—but checked out Ken—

only to find nothing—and that nothing

filled my hours and my days with promises
never made—yet something else quietly
stalked me through a gray maze of flesh painted

dreams—portraits of the dark—i did not know
what i sought in that park—it was a thing
built of shadow and need—it was secret—

                even to me

West Wind Rising
Arlene Downing-Yaconelli, Citrus Heights, CA

tucked inside
crumbled walls
a church yard

overgrown
cypress and cedar
shade cold stone

wind-scoured grey
lichened warriors
decked in drifting petals

worn away under
crisp crusts of granite
tilted monuments topple

ages old
entropy caressed
impermanent

beyond rusted gates
on mud-splattered tanks
shadows lengthen

twitch in a rising wind
launchers swivel
drones snarl the skies

casings clatter on
cracked pavement
the dead lie frozen
    shoeless

Dissonant Consonance
Maryann Wilkey, Kissimmee, FL

Like a shadow, grief won't release me, neither will love.
Say it isn't so, you transitioned, shattering my heart...
From a lifetime of love to a life sentence of grief;
You're unfettered and dancing, I'm bound and mourning.

Say it isn't so, you transitioned, shattering my heart.
Eternity in Paradise is yours to keep, Loss on Earth is mine to bear.
You're unfettered and dancing, I'm bound and mourning.
Ruminating on memories: your birth, your smile, your jokes, your allure.

Eternity in Paradise is yours to keep, Loss on Earth is mine to bear.
Death can't, death won't have the last word; Love has more to say;
Ruminating on memories, your birth, your smile, your jokes, your allure.
Valuing the least of us, embracing castaways, your trademarks live on.

Death can't, death won't have the last word; Love has more to say.
Grief and love battle for residence in my heart, both agree to remain.
Valuing the least of us, embracing castaways, your trademarks live on.
Like a shadow, grief won't release me, neither will love.

My Fourth Headstone
Olivia Channon, Manchester, NH

I find I'm drawn to graveyards, especially my own.

The cemetery is tucked out in the quiet corner of the backyard. A town of three headstones, with a new resident on order.

My first headstone is the messiest: a ruin showing its age.
It crumbled through a slow ending where I couldn't find the exit. Didn't know if there was a door.
After decades, I was finally escorted out of the house of expectations I would never meet.
I was dead long before I found this marker. I leaned on this stone to learn to breathe again.
It took years, but now the crocuses I planted here bloom all on their own.

My second headstone was laid frantically, in a panic.
It's tilted, off-center, and I spelled my own name wrong; I couldn't proof-read underground.
This death was a terrible surprise. A flash bang as the dirt opened up and swallowed me whole.
I wasn't the only one that died that day, but I was alone when I came back.
Every week on Tuesdays, I come to wipe off the layer of my anger that still collects like dust.

My third headstone is an odd shape - cinched in at the middle and dotted with divots.
"I hate you, I hate me, just please don't leave; stay, stay, please, just stay!" the inscription cries.

I knew the real message; I should have seen it sooner. Did, but closed my eyes.
Those gouges house my fingerprints, where I wrapped my arms tight and held on for too long.
This stone reads LONELY, and I've learned to love her above all the others.

My newest headstone will take this slot.
A 'Sold' sign swings over the open ground.
For the first time, I've had a hand in the funeral planning. I picked the flowers, know the venue.
I've chosen the perfect font for the carving: COMFORT KILLS; RISK REVIVES.
By welcoming grief with an invite, I get to choose where she sits at the service.
My fourth iteration will be buried under words about how I've finally learned to die a quiet death.

As dirt falls into the space, the last whispered critiques of leaving something safe for something
fulfilling will be snuffed out of earshot - especially those from myself.
I'll awake in my fifth life to the sound of mourning doves.

Live Laugh Love
Cindy Pruett, Scottsdale, AZ

LIVE
Ask a child, "What is life?"
and wait for the reply.
It's one big rollercoaster
that you ride until you die.

Ask an elder, "What is life?"
and listen close to hear.
It's learning from the ups and downs
and growing year by year.

Both have found the answer–
one by nature; one through time.
And though there may be twists and turns,
we choose to stand in line.

For life, it moves so quickly–
moments melt the years away.
Don't live thinking there's tomorrow–
make the most of every day.

LAUGH
Ask a child, "What is laughter?"
Wait for the retort.
It's a happiness exploding
from your tummy with a snort.

Ask an elder, "What is laughter?"
Listen carefully.
It's the body's way of letting out
its stored anxiety.

Both are right on target—
one is simple; one is deep.
And if you chuckle often,
how much better you will sleep.

For laughter, it can heal you—
making life seem more worthwhile.
It's the soul rejuvenating—
oh, how mighty is the smile.

LOVE
Ask a child, "What is love?"
and wait for what is said.
It's all about a warm embrace;
a cozy tuck in bed.

Ask an elder, "What is love?"
and listen to each word.
It's never letting fires die
by keeping embers stirred.

Both are filled with wisdom—
one that's given; one we learn.
It's the brightest flames that fizzle—
seek the slower, steady burn.

For love, it's never ending—
what you give is never gone.
Those you've touched will take the torch,
and in your honor, pass love on.

Further Than You've Ever Been
David Allen Sullivan, Santa Cruz, CA

Make of me an enzyme to catalyze
a conversion, roll me on the tongue
of your sermon, harp-string my heart
until the piercings break out in song,
pick ripening buds and light me up
so I can traverse your trachea, invade
your tiniest alveoli, be hinged on your
in-out-breaths, be death *and* life and
all you squeeze between those tight
parentheses—let me be what's in you,
what passes through, friend of fuck-
ups and what-ifs, gentle fulcrum file
wedging under pick-up-sticks of all
your missed opportunities—your
every lover stripped of clothes and
jealousies, long lost loves bi-folded
in my back pocket, I'm carrying you
further than you've ever been—trust
me, no need for off-ramps, rain-checks,
check outs, pills—we're making tracks
that don't double back, attacking
the naysayers with this fountain
of *yes-ands*, spilling out the crown
of your head, rooting down through
bare feet to soften every rocky bed.

Mettle (no clay)
Jacqueline Gryphon, Portland, ME

not from Adam's rib was i formed,
neither from bone, nor clay,
i am no *other* of Adam.

a succulent, teeming day it was
with the breath of leaves misting
and a soft breeze soughing by the lake-
when Greatness bent low,
and in generous, fullness of body
scooped from those waters,
a green lip of bulbous foam, rolling it along plump fingers,
and in gesture of design, bent lower yet again
to lift and mix--vine, twig, and loam,
whose rich humus joined earth and sky
and in greatest wisdom,
and joyous laughter
folded, shaped and caressed me, licked fingers
patting them to further form me,
before placing me in the universe of garden
where i bloomed
in image of all that was good.

how do i know all this about my origin?
i listened well.

The Walker
Elizabeth Hill, New York, NY

I write poems
Because my mother died,
Compelled,

Like my father
Accepts the walker
Pressed on him

By the aides
At the home, who say
Get him to try it.

His eyesight shrinks
Like the end of a
Looney Tunes cartoon.

The old folks croon
He is so popular here
With everyone.

Like my husband with his
Easy chatter on the
Work Zoom,

The way he too
Blithely navigates the
Difficult ones.

Day Care Center.
Each small child
Demanding something of me,

Saying *Read
This book now* or
Pick me up.

My father held my mother up
In a bear hug
While she hung limp.

She was hollow
At the end of the phone when
She told me she was dying.

I feel her presence
With the soft antennae
That I strangely have.

I see her around
The corner of my eye,
Beside myself.

She is so nearly
Present. Even the way
She sometimes was:

Your brother was the smart one.
Would she love my poems
Or compete with them?

When I am dead
Susan Lindsley, Decatur, GA

When I am dead
And what I was is scattered
In the daffodils,
I will no longer smell the coffee
In the morning
Or hear the bobwhite
Calling to his mate.

I will not feel the sunlight
Or turn my face to welcome falling snow.
I will not hear the kitten purr
Or feel her flex her paws in joy
Upon my chest.
I will no longer hear the hounds
Pursing possums or raccoons
And barking their delight
As they run across the ground
Where I am lying.

If I can never smell magnolias
Or the lilies
Or hear the music of the mockingbird
Or gobblers from the hills
Or feel the hoofbeats of the whitetails running by,
But if the human soul
Should live forever,
I pray whatever gods may be

To let mine stay
Where I have lived,
To roam the woods,
The meadows
And the streams,
To ride the mustangs,
Sail the winds,
And waltz with butterflies
On rainbows
To the songs of meadowlarks.

The Longing
Lillian Stroup, Great Falls, VA

Who are you?

A longing for a mythical hope.
Daydreams of unicorns, dragons,
And mysterious castles.
A silent throne room—
Two empty chairs await.

Who are you?

Distant,
Stars embedded in clouds.
Another missed trip around the sun.
Buried—the core of the Earth,
Burning hot, yet silent as death.

Who are you?

A gosling flapping weak wings,
Unable to fly South for the winter.
Grounded, lost, alone—
A flightless bird,
An unnatural weakness.

Who are you?

A question directed at stars for years—
Wishes to an empty throne.
A mental projection to the Earth's core.
A prayer to the Gods of flight.
Unanswered, unknown,
But still—hope awaits.

Perhaps you speak to the stars, too.
Wondering of a mysterious Queen,
The missing core of your world,
A pair of wings to help you fly.

I imagine you, as you are now,
Sighing at another hope lost,
Staring at the sky, only to ask:

"Who are you?"

Conversing with Moths
Alexandra Wurth, Sioux City, IA

The click of the answering machine sounded,
As I stood in the doorframe,
Darkness enveloped her whole room,
Dissolving her empty bed into the rest of the vacant space,

Her room held a stillness, an engulfing silence that was so loud
Only a child could hear its frequency,
Static played, followed by a distant voice I couldn't make out,
I swear that night I was conversing with an angel,

One with fresh wings, outstretched like a brand-new moth,
Feet clinging on to her cracked cocoon for just a moment
Before taking flight into the open night sky.

Ashes of our Past
Ellie Starr, Junction city, OR

ashes of our past
frozen in the red light-
while waving notes dance
on the pale wind;

we taste smoke
in our lungs
from a crimson sky,
brimming with passion
of a most peaceful kind,

now the song in the wind,
awakens Time
suddenly to turn an eye
on the wandering of mortal lives;

as we,
wrapped in vibrant
velvet light,
serenaded by violet songs
on infinite lines
-that Time draws
while she listens
to the coming and going
of our lives;

such thin lines...

My Visitor
Jere Truer, Yuma, AZ

The conquered spirit of depression arrived
Saying his one-word command: Stop.
I ask him if he is sad. "Not really
But you do not listen."
He points out he visits me when I lie
About who I am and how I am living.

"It is exhausting holding up your many
Masks and deceptions."
But I want to write like Neruda.
"But his spirit lived in a country
Which has not lost its soul.
Yours has not only lost its soul
But mocks the very idea of soul.
How can you be who you are?"

And so, I sit in my sad chair
In my sad room holding the small child
I once was before colonization.
"That's right," he says, "Mourn
And reclaim your sovereignty.
Then I will come no more."

The World is not a Loving Place
Kodi Gonzaga, Pasadena, CA

the world is not a loving place,
my parents told me to my face.
it is not kind, but cold and cruel,
and it will take you for a fool.
if you so much as smile wrong
or answer to a stranger's song
or whisper secrets to a friend
or try to bring about the end
or even try to run away
(a route i thought of every day),
the world will know and block your path,
and you will suffer all its wrath.
i wonder if they know the trick:
the world needs you to make it tick,
its lessons taught with words and fists,
with gentle eyes and laundry lists,
the world made flesh through flesh and bone
(eternal, you need not atone).
i cannot hate, for this they learned
through pain and punishments they earned.
one day i'll sit them down and sigh
and tell them it was all a lie
(a foolish trial, yes i know,
but i can't help but love them so).
until that point, so far away,
i'll carry on, and every day,
the people who meet me will find,
despite it all, the world is kind

I Only Remember Fireflies
Sandra Brown Lindstedt, Portland, OR

Crickets was having some kind of party
dancing and singing outside my window
music keeping me awake.
One song kept time with my heartbeat as I lay there—still.
The bed was damp with my sweat.

Waited for a breeze to wander in. It never came.
Wiped the palms of my hands
on clean, crisp white linen.
I heard whispering from the next room.

I waited for it to stop.
My fingers felt for creases in the sheet.
testifying of strength Grandma used when she ironed
pressing down hard, the edge of each pleat could cut you.
I was now at peace.
I was home.

Two day journey on the Amtrak train is now a memory.
All aboard, ma'am! All aboard ma'am! All aboard! Bound for Texarkana!
He lifted me up like a rag doll onto the platform
One AM. Lost my little red coin purse, changing trains in St. Louis.
Mama says we can't stop to look.

Finally. We arrive. I can breathe again
Finally. Chicago ain't got no more claims to me.
Finally. I close my eyes. Peace overwhelms me.

Tomorrow I will scrub grime and dirt of tenement ghettos off me.
It was clean under my fingernails and the roots of my hair.
The smells too.
Yes. The smell of drunk men's urine and cheap Wild Irish Rose wine
spilling down back alleyways
got all mixed together ending up at the bottom of our steps.
Tomorrow umma get clean.
Umma use Ivory soap Grandma keeps on the bottom cupboard shelf.
Umma take a bath in the big metal wash tub
hanging outside on the back porch. Yes.

Tomorrow umma skip down the dirt road to Aunt Hattie's house
sip sweet tea under her big shade tree.
Umma have all summer to swing on the rope behind the smokehouse
and chase chickens and catch fireflies,
and do whatever six year old girls do when they enter paradise
after being in hell.

Torchlight
August James, London, England

The forest closed in around me.
The trees, once welcoming,
now looked down, like decaying sentries.
Menacing.

The flowers, bright with gemstone colors,
now sprouted thistles the size of a shark's tooth.

Surrounded by darkness,
the sky filled with the rhythmic sound
of a dragon taking flight.

The only light, up ahead, in a clearing.
Torchlight, piercing the deep night.
The shadows danced and laughed.

I began, weaving a path towards the torchlight.
The sword at my back, catching branches sharp as broken glass.

I fell into the clearing, broader and deeper than expected.
Revealing two torches set on either side of a steal portcullis.

A dark castle loomed above, reaching toward a starless night.
Vines slithered up the black stone walls.
A single window flickered with candlelight high above.

As I approached, the gate opened with a slow, threatening creak, shattering the silence.

Here is the field
Candy Neubert, Cornwall, United Kingdom

If you don't lie down in a field now, then
when will you? Grass is important, you must
remember its rare smell. The stones and dust
and mice and ants will remind you of when
you used to lie down in the grass often
with arms outstretched and hugging the earth's crust,
feeling vertigo, learning how to trust,
how to be lifted up and dropped again.
Not here – it wasn't *this* field, but who cares
which? Listen to the crickets. Listen to
the crackle of the wind through the dry ears
whipping at the fences. Go on, push through;
lie down in the open like the wild hare.
If you don't do it now, when will you do it?

It's the End of the World
C. Oliver Watson, Overland Park, KS

it's the end of the world, and it's all everyone can talk about. someone's getting killed, someone's being brought to justice, someone's having their funeral. we're all connected, and we're all too close and we all know too much and we take it out on each other. someone is having a fight on twitter, on facebook, on some social media site. it's all we can do.

it's the end of the world, and all we can do is cry. no more happiness, no more birthday surprises, no more ice cream, no more holding each other. no more elections, no more fights on Thanksgiving, no more roasting the liberals, no more Twitter. no more joy, no more kisses, no more hugs, intimacy, laughter, love. someone screams that they're sorry. someone else screams for them to shut up.

it's the end of the world, and i'm doing my homework. i have a test on Monday, a project due Friday, finals in a month. i drive to work, i clock in, i work my shift, i clock out, i drive home. i eat, i sleep, i dream, i cry, i love. i scream that i love you. you can't look me in my eyes. it's the end of the world, and it doesn't matter. we're not the heroes, we're not the rich, we're going to suffer. so we might as well yell at each other in traffic, fight online, blame each other for things neither of us have done. nothings going to change.

it's the end of the world, and i'm tired. i'm so tired. everyone's tired. it's the end of the world, and capitalism doesn't stop unless everyone is dead. it's the end of the world, and rent is due on the 15th. it's the end of the world, and i can hear a bird singing, whistling.

it's the end of the world

Climbing Trees
Anna Paddick, Angola, IN

I did not have a childhood
My years were spent striving for an excellence
That I had no real hope of achieving
I was a child, after all
Though I didn't much act like one
I did not climb trees
I did not jump in puddles
I did not throw snow balls
I read
And I wrote
I mourn the little girl I could have been, wild and free
And I weep for the little girl I was, lonely and stuck inside
I spent my little years
Trying to grow up
Before the world would let me
And now that I have
I ache for when I was small
I honor both little girls
Who I could have been and who I was
I run home from little journeys
I dance in the rain
I walk outside barefoot
I admire even the tiniest of flowers
And
For both of their sakes'
And perhaps my own, too
I will climb a tree

Apples Have Nests
Elise Young, Brooklyn, NY

Flooding one continuous sphere that folds on itself.
The seeds of the apple, just stars in the sky.
Littering darkness like sweet juicy flesh
ripe with the vastness of the unknowing.
Let's dance on this seed? I say we shall.
And contort and sway and pulse.
This is all I want, filling up like a well it feels right.
How do we understand right if it is not by joy?
Plants feel joy in fact they are. True expressions
of gratitude reaching up to a source of joy,
oh please let me be a seed planted and reborn
again—an apple.
Streaks paint my skin and I feel the stem of my being.
If I feel, I also hurt. Bruised, bounding towards
Earth exiting this phase of my holiness,
I rest on death, but I am welcomed
Home—back to knowledge.
When I was in the air it felt sacred. Wind is holy,
it is so present when all you can be sure of
is your form and your size. Hello, thank you
for giving me this opportunity to dance.
Finally, I can be sure of my brothers and sisters.
Ground creatures and their young flood
the open wide while yellow and orange
note our arrival. Peering up at me
Creatures of the sky come and go,
dive and soar, they carry flesh in their mouths

through the holy wind.
Love is in their carefully collected nests,
it holds their young. If only apple's had nests,
we give our bodies over so air Creatures
have their flesh and their young beat on.
Loneliness exists here still, seeing
defines experience. Where you see,
I understand, but I am not rewarded for this.
Plucked from my shrine, tasked with
rotting. Decay is my only solace.
Mother says I am life and death's gift—all at once.
Darling soon I will be in your veins
absorbed with the help of joy source
in the meat of it all, it was a gift to be here

Cinnamon Skin
Samantha Paredes, Provo, UT

I was made in a factory like all the others.
Paraffin and pigment like everyone else.
I was melted from twenty different pinches of distinctly colored wax,
Not quite Native caramel but not African cocoa or French vanilla.

The other shades were easily identifiable by name and appearance:
Charcoal, Raspberry, Sunset:
Easily recognizable skins from variety packs.
I, the dusty, ruddy brown was drawn over with them,
never quite the correct shade for someone's fridge sketch.

The more common wax sticks were blended into lovely hues with their
own stories to tell.
Stories of candlesticks and mica, of pristine metal molds
and boxes shipped to the same country.
How did the little strange color end up in a box in Provo, Utah?
I fell out of my specialty box into a variety pack that was packed into the
wrong plane's compartment.
I was never meant to be here.

No one wanted me for art projects or leisurely doodles.
But perhaps my masterpiece is waiting for me.
One day, a little girl who's searching for her skin will find me.
She will weep for joy that there is a hue in that box that fits her
oddly specific shade.
She'll read the label on my paper dress and caress it lovingly.
"Cinnamon", she'll read.
"This crayon is for coloring Cinnamon Skin."

Nod to Eden
Mercy Haub, Shoreline, WA

A dark, soft film of ground does float away,
My sole's imprinted ghost returning home.
My weary feet undress and bow to pray,
Their charge with altered end of lighted roam.
I know the rivers carved into your knees
Have borne a young and muddy painting too.
Portraits of black and grey and brown and green
Connect me, though far away, back to you.
And with each cleansing gust of liquid sky
I eye each running speck and watch it go.
Without water all plants would surely die.
Adults forget that they need ground to grow.

Freedom
Bruce Clark, Wavell Heights, Australia

His wife and two small daughters,
both diminished by the wide-eyed amazement of departure,
sat with blank-faced stares behind the railway-carriage glass,
his face mirrored there for him, but only for him, outside.
Inside, they were already pond dwellers in an unknown new pond,
and he the outsider forbidden to breach the surface.
His wife's eyes spoke creeds of love,
though nobody could rightly speak anything at all.
Final hand-prints pressed against both sides of the glass,
freely seen, but unsealed, seared their new separation,
a new graffiti, as horrid diesel dragged their worlds apart.
Fear locked his heart.
Without him, they were on their way to freedom.

The weapon was a toy in his gentle hands,
foreign as invasion to this thoughtful, docile man.
These hands had gestured the air with fervour
as the literature of Life, the poetry of the World,
had transposed from this passionate custodian
into the smiling faces of each new year of tenants.
The smiles were often patronising; youthful arrogance.
Yet the memory was implanted, of the content and the man.
Each grain of truth empowered their unbound futures. Unlike he,
who now fired his first-ever round of death at an anonymous outline.
Future for them was yet an uncharted map, and borderless.
Their only invasion theirs as they stepped free to journey.
Their only invoice his wisdom to be mined.
Without him, they were on their way to freedom.

The frenzy of the fire-fight intensified as he approached,
a member of an untrained brigade undeserving of the name,
but directed into action by a citizen officer equally as bereft as they.
They scattered for cover as the first volleys zinged close,
wide-eyed beasts encountering the first-time brutality of a branding iron.
Targets were nothing more than the tell-tale source of firing,
confrontation too abject to risk, too foreign to master now.
His first vision of a properly badged and uniformed enemy,
an invader spitting indiscriminate death into ill-discerning civilians,
came complete with a huge apparatus designed only to deliver oblivion.
Striding boldly into the open, this enemy fired down the shelter of an alley.
A mufti-clad young body toppled out to sprawl in the antiseptic snow,
the dead face, once lively with charm in his classroom, now only dead.
The amused arrogance of the soldier engendered no retaliation
when the untrained shooter shoved an untrained gun at his chest, and fired.
The blasted enemy was now as dead as his blasted student.
The needlessness of both steeled a shield about the shooter's heart.
He strode forward, demanding angry revenge.
Without heart, he was on his way to freedom.

Truth or Consequences, New Mexico
Morgan Smith, Santa Fe, NM

Sliced apples, a bag of pecans and
a pale New Mexico sky
as we head south past Truth or Consequences.
But there is no truth anymore.
Only consequences.
It's 57 degrees on
April 17 as we share these snacks.
All we have is each other.
Maybe that's the only truth.

An Epitaph is Enough
Maryann Russo, Palos Verdes, CA

Here lies *Enough*, who lived a long life that never measured up.
Now the glass is void of its red delineations. I can see clear
through to the contents. My intelligence will not be marred
by Einstein, or my altruism, by Mother Theresa. No longer
will my body be discounted by Kardashian curves or gravity.
Without Enough, time gets to spread out, stretch its wide wings.
It can fly unfettered. Good gets to shine, wherever it shows up,
just as it is, a moon crescent glimmer, tipsy in the sky, or in its
full ripe splendor. *Enough* never has to arrive as an interruption–
my sentence can go on, the speech can go on, this poem can go on,
or decide to stop on a half word. A life can keep going, into a room
not yet seen, eons past Hope. And Love—Love can suspend its
discrimination, forsake the pick and choose.
Without *Enough*, Love can become everything.

The Back Wall
Matthew Ratz, Kensington, MD

The elements of the human spine are bones,
cartilage, and nerves; any contraction
or disc displacement
slips the paths of our ability to feel
and cuts off our very humanity.

This thought strikes me
as I glance at the upright spines
of ancient tomes along the back wall
of our used book store.
Are book spines akin to our own vertebrae?
If we opened the pages of ourselves
and spread our margins wide
like a yawning lung,
would we remain stitched up in the center?
Our breath cascading like the fragile pages
of this 17th-Century handbook on
children's respiratory infections
I gently restore to its nook.

Did you know there's a company downtown
endeavoring to 3D print a human lung?
My chest is cavernous like these stacks,
and my heart is delicate
as that vintage art book you cradle
in your palms.
Oh to be dog-eared in your library!

To be poured over by lamplight
in your scholarly pursuits.

The effervescent joy of watching you bend
close to my pages,
catching the rarest phrase
as it seizes your breath.
To shop with you along every back wall
of the book stores of the World,
a treasure hunt across time.

There is a bookstore in Iraq
where books are left out overnight.
They say thieves don't read
and readers don't steal.
Such is the sanctuary of you for me
where all is just and fair.
To sip the chalice of this forgone wisdom
beside you
is to taste ambrosia.

Light Frozen Deep in the Ice
Clif Mason, Bellevue, NE

Did we miss the flock of crows?
It came & went like a sound bite.
What have they done
with the pitchfork?
It's missing from the painting.
Whole cities filled are with vacancies.

The absences are palpable.
We run into them wherever we go.
Every loneliness
is lonely in its own way.
When all the public faces meet
in a park, no one sees

the faces beneath.
If all the family truths are packed
away in attics,
people have no choice
but to dress in myths.
Life becomes a missing person.

Investigators hold out little hope.
The world is filling
with shallow graves.
Light frozen deep in the ice
of insidious custom—entombed
throughout the Holocene—

has been set free, has become
new words intoned by a vast
invisible mouth, words that move,
in the capillary action of radical
thought, through the minds
& spirits of the bereaved,

the burnt hearts of the disconsolate,
bringing ice-searing release
at last from tests
they couldn't hope to withstand,
a joy as unexpected
as it is unsurpassed.

Playlist
Tara Zafft, Saint Louis, MO

This year for my birthday, I did something different. I asked
my children for what I wanted. Really, wanted. I asked

for something created. Something intentional, something not
bought. And my eldest called me on my birthday, my Tel-Aviv afternoon,

her DC on the way to work morning. And she said,
Happy Birthday, and she said, *check your texts Maman;*

I just sent you a playlist. She told me that every song was deliberate,
and the order was too, and that I must listen to it all at one time.

So I did, the next morning, on my morning Boardwalk walk. I listened
for meaning in words, tried to sense signs, intertwined

by my child who doesn't always say what she feels, to me,
her mother-poetess. But my clear-thinking child had me in tears two steps

in with the first line of the first song. About a mama who *gave everyone
her light.*

And just then, as if on purpose, as if God had timed the sun to blind
my sight,

I knew she saw me. The way mamas crave to be seen, the way we cry at night
because we try but get it wrong, because we try again the next day,

but get it wrong, again, only in a different way, our words
are our words and then they are not our words, we are wanted, and then

not wanted, and all we want is for our babies to know we love them.
To know we once were their age, idealistic, determined to be

the best version of a mama, that somehow, we never achieve. But I knew, now
she saw. And it was all okay. We'd be ok. And I knew, I could stop the
playlist right at that

moment, because I had found the Holy Grail. But, I kept going. Because
she asked. Because I promised. Because I was enjoying the invitation to
pay attention. To words.

And then to salty air. And then to morning joggers, like the old Israeli
jogging-man

wearing a t-shirt saying *Triggered.* Did he know what it meant? The songs wove

together our family history, of schools in France and Bali monsoons. Of
teenage silences

and college in New England. Of Appalachia in my blood and Missouri
in hers. And I saw a

mother and adult daughter, nearly matching camel-colored raincoats,
squeeze-embracing.

The daughter turned to go and pulled a strand of her mother's hair from
her mouth. They

laughed. These women, mother and daughter woven together. Am I, like them, my daughter and me? And I wonder is everything intentional? Like the playlist? Like the mother and

daughter? I am blessed, and I think how strange it is that *blessed* looks like the French word for wounded, *blesses*, and I wonder if the magic of feeling blessed is born from woundedness, the

hollow-ache of aloneness. A man, alone, well dressed in leather jacket and light-blue scarf knotted at the neck, that made him look European, had two exact shoes of two different colors.

Why? I wondered as he wandered, as I wandered. A very pregnant woman paused, then

leaned on her partner, then held her belly. She breathed. I breathed, and I

remembered the first contraction of my first child, my go-getter, my playlist-maker. When I

held my blueberry bran muffin at a café in London, and thought, is this it? The beginning

of a life? The moment it begins? I still remember her eyes. Blinking, quiet, we looked

at each other. She was my world, still is. Wait, the doctor said, *for the cord to stop pumping;*

let her get everything she needs. Did she get everything she needs? I put my hand on her newly born belly. Felt her heart. She was magic. She is magic. And this playlist. Magic.

Lorde saying she doesn't want to be angry anymore, and the Truck Band saying let's love

now, and the one that says this is a long-distance love. But my baby is wrong.

There is no distance. *Revival*, the last song seals, but really, reveals, just another

beginning. The singer thanks the band, says we couldn't make music without you.

Five Seasons
Daniel Carroll, Gaithersburg, MD

When summer's end resembles spring,
Autumn waits while nightingales sing
      Delightful tunes to a deceitful breeze.
And morning's dew refreshes the air,
Whose sweet caress lessons my cares.
In singular moments hope trumps despair.
      There's time to stand at ease.

Until yellow, orange, and red fall in,
To tune Vivaldi's violin,
      And draw out tired green.
Blazing colors now dazzle my eyes,
While grays and blues court in the skies,
Over shortened days that still surprise,
      With grandeur, ever serene.

Sentry winter descends in due order,
Tossing fall, holding no quarter,
      Threatening never to leave.
Naked limbs sway in the wind,
And brace themselves when cold sails in,
Sweeping beige and white in air so thin,
      Painting shadows there to grieve.

Yet radiance returns in gentle strips,
Loosening winter's insistent grip,
Flowering spring's encore.
Green peaks up and steals the show,
Brushing aside remnant snow,
To weave the season of blush and glow,
My spirit to restore.

After a year and six hours,
Summer reasserts its power,
Devouring delicate spring.
Landscapes scream in flush attire,
The Heavens counter with cannon fire,
Showering relief at day's retire,
For blissful rest as crickets sing.

Around its star, with tilt and spin,
May our celestial sphere traverse again,
Forever, until the end of time.
For my part, while enduring this life,
Its manifest struggles and hidden strife,
Small tribute to God's glory may it suffice,
This thanks for five seasons Divine.

Between Two Shores
Lynne Burnett, Parksville, Canada

Like a great wind, scattering leaves and debris
before him, shaking pale, folded blossoms
from slender parental branches, raging against
the doors and windows of neat, contained houses,
my son comes bellowing into adolescence.

This is the mighty breath of a warrior god
blowing through him, emptying him suddenly
of his quiet, rapturous ways, gripping his
hands and limbs and pulling him dangerously
fast down open roads, over vast unpatrolled seas.

I want to hold him back—a puer aeternus—
and keep his hand in the cookie jar,
the tulips swooning in their vase,
uplifted by the merest breeze of his passage
through the golden rooms of summer,

the hours ours to confide in—a pond ripple
of minnows silvering the lazy afternoon
or seized, hockey sticks clashing in the carport,
my bedtime stories still believed, letting the hero
awake while the swordless boy sleeps.

But no. He is already swimming past me
into the white-capped future. Between two shores
he raises an arm and crawls, stroke by stroke,
toward the lit horizon. I grieve his footprints
disappearing from the sand.

He bends an ear—so deep the liquid notes
that lift and drop him, so willing the instrument
he has unwittingly become.
In that god's determined hands, there will be
no return from the journey begun.

Life Lesson
Dianne Ochiltree, Sarasota, FL

Life will break your heart if you let it.

Don't.

Life will bend you, give to you, take from you.

The plot thickens, the villain appears, the lover arrives, the triumph is won, the prize is lost.

In all this, remember:

Hold fast to your heart.

Follow it faithfully.

Protect it fiercely.

For it's the pen with which you must write your story.

Sailing
Glenn Moss, New York, NY

Sliding from leaf, slipping into the water with a soft tongued kiss

Sunlight ripples the river's surface flashing coded messages

Moving with the current, like the hips of a familiar lover

Tempted, so tempted, to step in, untie from fears and drift

No oars or compass needed

From one bank, blood from a severed throat flows like sap

From the other, corpses with rotting violins playing like Venuti and Grappelli

Branches become fingers point,

then curl and beckon promising sharp nailed pleasure

Once, those fingers felt like answers to questions I didn't ask

Today, my answer is to untie and enter the river

Direction uncertain, an egret slaps the water creating ripples I will follow

for a while

Maybe I'll end up in the Bay of Fundy or in Lisbon

Sweat becomes a sail of laughter

The Road

Brooks Carver, Canton, IL

Dirty face with dark, hollow eyes,
Looked no more than about twelve.
The breeze brought his sour, sweaty smell
Blowing in through the screen door.

Baggy pants shredded, too large,
In desperate need of mending.
He wanted work but food mostly.
Janey made him wash at the well
Then fed him cornbread and cold milk.

The boy finished off the afternoon
Helping Sam cut fence posts.
Janey could see from the porch
Across the pasture to the edge
Of the timber that the strokes of his ax
Were weak, ineffective, feeble.

Supper was quiet, subdued, cheerless.
He spoke not a word but *thank you,*
A little more, all right, and please.
Then, fell asleep on his empty pie plate.

Sam carried him to the porch
Wrapped in an old blanket.
A soft, raggedy pair of overalls
Under the boy's head for a pillow.

The next morning
The porch was empty.
Boy, blanket, and overalls
Gone west with the dawn.

Janey stood for awhile
Staring down the road.
Somewhere, a mamma is
Grieving for her boy, she said.
I hope nobody steals the
Dollar I put in his pocket.

Aeneas
Everett Roberts, West Hollywood, CA

Did you hear my
voice? I could not stop calling for you.
Far ahead of me, I see nothing golden
Though I remembered all the tales,
The branch I broke could bring me close
to you again, or so I was told
The last words fate lets me say are these:
Please don't leave me. I have seen
sweetness ahead. I do not want
to savor it alone

Lament—I cannot pretend any longer, have I lost my
Way out— deep within the wood I wander,
Do I turn back, admit defeat, and understand I am beaten?
I did not know a story was all that would remain.
Try to see me as you once did. I have come
to prove how powerless I always was.
Somehow I did not love you enough. I failed you. And yet,
the golden bough still glimmers, it's enough to try again, I see
this path. This was our time, a memory is not enough, and
can never be enough.

I will tell myself this lie forever.

Dirt
Barbara Scoblic, Bethesda, MD

Cleaning dirt from under my fingernails
before dressing for the prom
Mud oozing between our toes wading in the river
Dirt in the creases of my father's forehead
Mud, sucking strong, impossible to drive through
Moist dirt mounded above my mother's grave
Dirt frozen too hard to take my father's coffin
Dirt
Damned dirt
Blessed dirt

As I Was
Malik Jones, Juneau, AK

I went for a walk one harsh winter evening. The mid-season snowflakes were wide as eyes, beaming at the looming furnace dressed in black.

My breath the stage for snowflakes' dance, they pranced until my coat turned white.

Just past the edge of streetlight's reach, groaned a breeze, hollow and bleak; a cutting howl thought almost speech, or even query.

"Have you come to join me?" My outreached hand a gentle please. The mind seeks company, even in lonesome reprise.

Perhaps it was a moose, the bears should be asleep. With heed well taken my mind could wander more.

I marched again the darkened breach. Cold playfully snapping at my heels and tapping at my nose.

I miss the nights of wildfire green, painted in streaks across the sky. But settled for the frostbit air, pinching at my cheeks and tugging at my clothes.

Until beside me walked a figure. Stalking, baulking at my brooding form. An absence in periphery, a gap among the snow.

Mockingly, I asked, "Are you some ghost born of my past, come to teach a moral that I lack?"

No answer came, no sounds were made, save those hollow groans, persisting of the wind.

The figure's gaze it did not shift. Blizzard spun around the shape,
apprising of its space.

Awkwardly I raised my pace. Around a corner it gave chase.

"What do you want, an apology?" Which haunting wrong should I
make right?

Cold no longer nipping at my feet but biting sharp with many teeth. A
numbing, angry, heat. A malice marrow deep.

I must move forward, can't turn back. Is that the lesson that I lack?

Another turn, I thought it lost. Though winter's scorn does not know brevity.

My gait cut trenches in the snow, which piled higher as I slowed. My toes
too cold to recognize severity.

No windows lit, no witnesses. Before me it was stood. The chilling void
where winter should have been.

"You are not real," ghostly foe. This woe is my own reverie, this pain is
mine to feel.

With shoulders back and level chin, I stayed on track and met the devil.

Snowflakes kept their distance, as they danced around the figure dressed
in black.

Stood chimney tall with steaming breath and spreading winter grin. A
furnace lit with newfound yearning.

A pointed torch on midnight journey.

He Loves Me Not
Alyssa Hickey, Port Saint Lucie, FL

My loneliness knocked again today,
To see if I was still plucking flower petals—
He loves me, he loves me not, he loves me.
It shook its head at me, softly beckoning,
"Come inside," it pleaded, shaking.
"The skies are gray, and it is going to rain."

My loneliness wrapped its arms around me,
Trying to chase away the empty space,
But it was so cold—like the blue of your eyes
Or the stillness in our kitchen on your bad days.
We both waited - holding our breath
As if silence would give us the answers.

My loneliness sat with me today, as always,
Filling the void where you were supposed to be.
It stroked my hair and read me stories of
romance and butterflies, and a deep sweeping love
— as if to remind me that was not who I loved.

My loneliness cried today, with big, shaking sobs,
Rattled by your lack of affection — Not even one hug.
It whispered, "Sweet girl, you deserve a hug today,
But you'll have to find it some other way."
And as the rain and thunder started,
I was left to remain

To Marni
Cindy Glovinsky, Ann Arbor, MI

Child of storms, never to be tamed,
unbreakable piebald filly—
You taught us what we could not do.

Needing so much more than anyone
could give, giving all you had to
those who gave back nothing.

Street-smart and tattooed,
wielding your high voice like a rapier,
you loved homeless men, animals, babies.

We were so different, you and I:
You loved heavy metal, I loved Debussy;
You loved horror movies, I loved Jane Austen.

But we both loved your dad.

Little by little, we had to fight past
vampire dreams and slammed doors,
past wicked stepmothers and mean sisters,

Past unkind words like poisoned apples,
past hunger and padlocks and flares and ice,
past fears with eyes as big as saucers,

To arrive, finally, at this friendly communion
over pork dumplings, in the company
of two good men.

When the Bough Breaks
Sammi LaBue, Brooklyn, NY

It was, for so long, a wild kaleidoscope of life:
Dive bombing swallows,
Swarms of yellowjackets,
Slime green caterpillars disappearing into tiger striped butterflies.
We almost forgot to believe in grief.
Rib cage became birdcage
Became twelve arms on each side of our hearts for gathering,
And there was so much to take:
Kale growing faster than you could wilt it down in a pan,
Blackberry bushes too tall to pick from,
Mowed grass looking ragged the very next day.
And then, as if all of a sudden, the moon was full,
So big shining light on the immensity of all that life
It looked like it might fall from the sky.
The next day, we were full of noticing, too:
A nest unfinished, left half woven to fall from a tree,
Turkey feathers and daisy petals, picked off like wishes by a harsh wind,
And one bright red leaf on the trail, so pretty.
A coyote, all alone, howling,
Begging the summer not to end.

The water is lower in the stream now,
And a bird sits in it, exhausted, remembering.
Remembering that living is never just living.
She looks at me, as if to say,
It's a mixed bag, isn't it?

But even as the water slips away,
Time comes around to fill the banks up again.
And us,
And the bird
Who is shaking her feathers dry,
Eating overripe blackberries that she doesn't have to fly for
Knowing there will be another time where the earth riots next year.
There will be another nest
When a hard rain falls, shaking the right twig loose,
And something feels worth wanting enough to fly for again,
Gathering it up.

God of Me
Joanne Gram, Lansing, MI

The god of me is not a jealous god
but may be self-centered at times
tending to self-care while taking care
to avoid trampling on other beings
sheltering the nests of ducks
and the caverns of hanging bats
The god of me takes pride
in creating beauty   recycling trash
building monuments to natural
spaces made of golden leaves
without montary concerns
The god of me sings love into the universe
holding the high notes for extra beats
sending a riot of colors after a drenching rain
The god of me maintains an identity
and an integrity easily gracefully
presenting personal power in the face
of adversity and dares to dream out loud

Hand Me Downs
Wanda Courville, Eunice, LA

You never own a hand-me-down.

It inhabits your world.

It's neither friend nor foe.

You tolerate it like an umbrella

That you carry on a rainy day.

It was never your choice.

You long for the day when you can discard it.

The operative, piercing word is "need".

You needed it because your family couldn't supply it.

Your pride is bruised.

It seems to own you.

Finally, through abiding grace you realize

That it was never about owning – just receiving.

Perfect Days: A Sonnet for Gary
Eileen Valentino Flaxman, Green Valley, AZ

You were not perfect. In truth, nowhere near.
Nor I. Not even on a perfect day.
I'd come. I'd go. But it's now become clear
Exactly why I decided to stay.
What you gave to me cannot be measured.
You kept the spark in me molten alive,
That part you insisted must be treasured
And so never let me forget that I've
The priceless gift of Imagination!
Hold it tenderly in your hands, you'd cry.
Breathe into it passion, inspiration…
Then watch it rise and shimmer in the sky.

      So, yes, I stayed. I let you light our way.
      And those were perfect, oh so perfect, days.

Ragdoll
Matthew Wilson, Racine, WI

Precious little ragdoll
They dragged you around
And tossed you to and fro

I saw your stitches tear
Saw your stuffing tumble out
It trails wherever you go

You'll be nothing soon,
Sweet ragdoll

Burial Ground
Eddi Salado, Ventura, CA

Again I return
to exhume the bodies of
your past lovers. To

caress their long white
bones under the Milky Way,
The Seven Sisters,

I imagine your velvet
kisses and spongy passion
with each one, touching

faces, winding curls
between your fingers, the
rosy ceremonies,

the sticky vows, and
rings that are buried deeply
away in this place

until the red blossoms
begin blooming through my blouse
spread peonies, roses,

and I know my heart
has finally bled enough

It is time to leave

and scrape the dark dirt,
Skin and bone beneath my nails.

I want my shoulder pain back
Ramiro Castro, Surrey, United Kingdom

Five cotton balls seek shelter in my hand. Faulty grip.
I polish nursery rhymes with excessive cream and wax. Running late,
rambling on about dinosaurs with no reciprocity, steering wheel to the left.

Five cotton balls go further and carry Peppa Pig plasters. Better grip.
My hand turns on Radiohead and muffles explicit screams. Shoulder pain,
numb mind, short attention span, giving way.

Five cotton balls blossom into tumbleweeds and roll across the front seat.
Flawless grip.
My hand cranks up Alan Walker's singles. Who is that?
I'm a mobile Freud with a major in school whining and a flat tyre.

The cotton season draws to a close after two thousand days of harvesting.
Five hairy sausages grip my shoulder while arriving at the last school assembly.
My hand now clutches the vacant seat, disoriented and rootless. I don't
need too much fuel anymore.

Fifteen cotton balls comfort my hand. I get a grip on myself.
In bed, I harvest flowers, plants, and ice cream. What's my name?
Five hairy sausages fluff the pillow as I steer towards the last terminal.
Time drives me away.

Boulanger's "D'un Vieux Jardin (of an old garden)"
Susan Hunter, Plymouth, MA

We hear a friend play the piano
against a windowed gray sky.
We look at the branches of large trees
holding the solid gray in their limbs.
We crane our necks to see a
pattern against the bleakness.

Can you hear the green gardens of Rome,
endless sun and fountains splashing with water?
The notes rise and rise, buoyed by dancing measures
and large green leaves.
Then, just unable to stay afloat, the notes fall
past the garden's marble cherubim, pot-marked by the years,

The girl, Boulanger, would die four years after writing the music.
She, dead against branches cutting a solid gray sky into pieces.
My friend plays her notes that hold the hope of laughing water,
children running circular paths in the garden.
The music vaults higher and higher,
before cascading with the rainwater
that has bathed this land all spring.

Our misting faces turn upwards,
then down to the piano keys.
Each note rises to the branches,
holding the sky for sun.

The Butterfly Fallacy
Madalyn Chevalier, Goose Creek, SC

Consider the butterfly and how she lives,
quickly, violently, passionately.
Twisting and writing,
she rips apart, transforming.

She emerges weak and delicate.
One touch and her wings will wither and tear.
Floating at the mercy of the wind,
she is a feather on the gusts of fate.

And yet in all this she sucks the flowers dry,
stealing their sweetness.
Developing a taste for blood,
iron and brutal on her tongue.

So when you see her flutter by
think not of grace and fragile beauty.
Think of the ferocity with which she lives,
the savage monarch of the skies.

The Water Bowl
Joseph Ridgway, Marlton, NJ

I'll see you somewhere in Dreamland,
somewhere in Dreamland tonight.
Murray Mencher and Charles Newman (1936)

Is that you again,
Softly drinking in
My dark hallway?
Your chain collar
Lightly striking your
Metal bowl—
A sweet concert
Of bells—
Unknowingly
Satiating my need
To hear your pleasure—
Impossible it is,
As you are now gone.
It is only
Dreamland again—
My heart
Thirsting once more.

Sunflowers
Mariah Reynolds, Palisade, CO

Two cut sunflowers,

withered and limp,

relinquish their seeds,

where morning rain penetrates the earth.

A slow reincarnation

encapsulating both life and death.

A moment where grief simply cannot exist.

Lachrimae Melancholia
Kimberly Joyce Heaton, Orem, UT

Pride won't concede a love that was lost.
How swiftly, how swiftly, Words Sever a Soul.
Bloodied and b r o k e n and never made whole.
The price much too high; humility the cost.

Waylaid by the seashore of unresolved fears.
A Siren's song calls, from the deep and the mist.
Beckoning. Beckoning, you, into the abyss;
maligning then drowning you in an ocean of tears.

Converted. Diverted. Subverted expectations.
We think ourselves clever, perspicacious, erudite.
and yet, ne'er acknowledge the blade or the point?
'less we awake, rise up, and make reparations.

Will we fall into the pyre and greet demons of unrest?
Or are we deferential to angels and heavens great light?
Some say this, some say that. Heaven or Hell be our plight!
We RAGE on and rage on, till we conclude life's brief test.

The Fever of a Black Shadow
Colin Dawson, Las Vegas, NV

And I sing into the white throat of an empty-hearted breeze,
dancing in the setting eyes of an autumn afternoon.
O I was born in the fever of a black shadow,
crying tears of dust across the yellow cornfields
in an old Ohio sky. O Ohio, spread your dark wings of ash,
and sing my song, everlasting, through the paraphernalia
of a dead red afternoon, with dying hands of rain
falling forever through the spirits and the ghosts
that walk on whispers of shadows,
through the bleached-white bones of prayers
and the pale roots of hope that shiver in a brand-new morning.

Tipsy Tongue
Nicola Lambo, Woodland Hills, CA

It's at your fingertips,
the words are forming on your lips.
The bell has rung, while the declaration sits there,
fuming on the tip of your tongue.
Your heart is racing, you're feeling defeatist,
veins ice cold, thoughts of out-of-touch elitists.
Fingers involuntarily start typing furiously across the keys
and suddenly you freeze...
But only for a moment, a moment you'll regret
when you hit send and it hits "the net".
While you downward spiraled, drunk on rage,
your rant went viral, every single page.

In retrospect, you should have waited,
now everyone weighs in on how they all hated
or felt elated, it's so contradictory, the whole things negated.
Now that you're deflated, "I'm angry" seems overrated,
not the slightest bit necessary or worth what it bated.

Some words are better left unsaid,
to marinate a little longer inside of our head.
Now your filled with dread as you recall,
The people you named, and you named them all.
Your fate is sealed, the axe will fall.
"Mirror, mirror on the wall?" you call.
Radio silence confirms your worst fears.
There are "no take backs" here.

It's ironic how socials are brutal, you begging and pleading, futile.

You know because you've been at it for a while.

But, give it a minute, trust that He's in it.

He'll rearrange some stuff.

In the mean time, things might get rough.

You stepped on some toes, you got redirected,

a meaning is in there it just got deflected.

The lesson is being made painfully clear,

pause when you find it difficult to hear

reason, it may not be the timing or even the season.

Don't be too hasty in your pursuit,

pull weeds out your garden, right at the root.

Patience is a virtue. Slow down, going too fast, may just hurt you.

If you're climbing, popularity isn't a goal, keep your eye on the ball,

It's the "Seat of the Soul".

The Princess
Daisy Campf, Summersville, WV

Silk, satin, and lace,
the princess wore the finest garments,
for she was a princess after all.
Oak, velvet and goose down,
the princess dreamt her dreams in luxury,
for she was royalty after all.
Commands, stares, and sarcasm,
the princess knew not to protest,
for she was a girl after all.
Tears, concealer, and smiles,
the princess never broke character,
for she was perfect after all.
Blood, bruises, and stitches,
the princess couldn't complain,
for she was lucky after all.
Ribs, mirrors, and collarbones
the princess had the perfect figure,
for she was beautiful after all.
Whispered prayers, muffled cries, silent screams,
grinding teeth, blistered skin, broken nails,
smeared mascara, stained ball gowns, shattered scales,
reaching arms, shaking hands, longing eyes,
the princess had a coveted life,
for she had it all.

All Things Must End (even Death)
Kerry O'Shea, Singapore, Singapore

Silence has a sound.
A low buzz,
a hiss that whispers of
the dense interwovenness of things.
At times,
the disinterest shown us
by the material
and spiritual worlds
seems almost wilful.

Gold Stars (for Branch, always a stellar artist)
Hilda Downer, Sugar Grove, NC

The refrigerator's own gravity
pulled the magnetic chart to its chest
where the center of its heart
was a gold star—
next to a chore
my three year old had completed that day.
The sticker booklet, flipped through,
wildly flashed red, green, blue, and silver,
juxtaposed by the basic colors in the crayon box.
Color occupied my son while I cooked.
In a booster seat at the countertop,
even then, he drew tractors and cats
that looked like tractors and cats.

Soon, the chore chart was swept away—
my energy drained by two jobs.
Amid abandoned wish lists for groceries,
exhausted coloring books,
unpaid bills, broken crayons, depleted pens,
and illegible notes for unwritten poems,
the star stickers washed up.
All the gold ones were gone,
leaving rows of white star teeth,
smile after smile.
The intact metallic colors braced tight,
fearful of giving up.

On the countertop edge,
gold stars held hands as far as they could reach
from the booster seat—
lined up like words on a fortune cookie banner
inside the dream
to live free as an artist
in a world inside a galaxy
my son had already created for himself.

Wounded Hands
Sheldby Schrock, Flower Mound, TX

i think i truly gave you
what heart i had left
you were my rock
you held my broken pieces
and cut your hands
so often
trying to put them back together
but you were not enough
you shouldn't have to be
my everything
you attempted to put all
the pieces back together
when some of them were lost
so long ago
it was impossible
and i couldn't accept your
inability to do everything
for me
and that was not your fault.
your love was just so beautiful
and so intoxicating
that i drank myself stupid
thinking it would never end.

Poem is Born
Gretchen Wiegand, Boulder, CO

Inkiness
Planets of words
Galaxies of phrases
Sparked by creativity
Seed planted
Fertilized by inspiration
Gestated in the mind
Infinite possibilities
Umbilical cord of knowledge
Composition growing
Urgency to express
Nurtured into being
Pushed out
Caught by hands of time
Essence released
Illumination
Composition of verse
Poem is born

Red Poppies
Susan Zwingli, Richmond, VA

The day your heart was silenced
somewhere, red poppies opened to the sun
a hundred vermillion kisses, warmth unfolding, promising
your light will not go out

City

David Saccone-Braslow, Southold, New York

It's all of you I want to be,

Not me.

I want to write off the page,

Or be written off the page,

Either serenity or a casualty.

Even awkward and ugly,

Like Dostoevsky and Bukowski.

Sure as a pothole,

Writers run streets.

In a world where pens are north stars,

And pages, nativities,

We fly around trying to tweet with Longfellow's beak.

Up in the lighthouse, read close,

And you can still hear Virginia weep.

How did she face the hours alone?

Was it love?

Or insanity?

Will it take a pocket full of stones to keep me in the seat?

Essay on the Failings of Memory
B.D. Olivier, Oxford, United Kingdom

I came from a town by the sea, where, all,
it seemed, of my father's life was lived. Fields
were my mother's home, where exceptional
nights were whole. I have friends, roofs and ideals,

a view of sky above it where the stars
belong to me, marking limits that shine
and break intimately in Afrikaans
in the tree-shadows as it draws its line;

fullness of a field; an everlasting rose
to which I have only myself to give.
And the trees do not die although it shows
how I'd walked this beach in exile, to live

where clouds bring their forefathers. Here I see
one who cries with the crying of a rage
living by all my days through history.
It was here, through the deep, gravel of ways

I walked; and through the disquiet sung
by plants; through the ruminating wind-sounds
where in a building I lettered in this tongue;
to learn to craft space with the words I found

at the central hurts of my life; forests
of wakening in love-memories
echoing through a time. But it warrants
visions and joyous mornings; centuries

of refracting crypts of thought that alights
where the dark will clang. But how I am just
a simile that won't rise to the heights
of metaphor, to burning change, and thrust?

How am I to live in a poem, I stroll
asking my scatterings? Meanwhile, outside
the streetlight, at my window, on its pole
keeping vigil, buzzing, won't sleep with wide

flames of heat readying. O how they stack
themselves to commit their acts of love ere
at every felled clearing, it'd mouth the black
change in your name. There I lived, there, there, there.

All Things
Anna McDermott, Boulder, CO

In the absence of understanding … intuition
In the absence of intuition … God
In the absence of God … Hope or despair
Step by step
Ignorance – awareness
Awareness – denial
The Loop – The Trap!
Over and over
Small miracles … vison, sight
Translation
Hidden languages
Interpretation
Love
All souls
All things
Connected
Love

Roots

Claudia Farese, Madrid, Spain

The thing about our roots
Is a matter of transition;
A land we once abandoned,
may shoot its weeds on upwards,
And clot the body vessels.

Such solid roots remind us
of oaks and elms so solemn-
Obliterate the sight
Of all the willows, weeping
on that stained riverside.

Old roots will cut the growth
of saplings towards light,
May steal their sleep at night;
A weight that speaks of debt,
Of depth, of rage, of Time.

Shuffling
Peter Ungar, Budapest, Hungary

A single sound infiltrated the kitchen,

the sound of repeated and approaching shuffling,

"why does the pavement not stick to your feet forever",

sitting in the kitchen someone could have thought,

but nobody thought things anymore

as the shuffling grew louder,

the lights became colder and bolder,

the smells disappeared completely,

less and less dust was left in the air,

when the shuffler reached the door and pressed the handle,

the room inside resembled a newly renovated clinic,

the kitchen that once smelled of diatomaceous earth

was now sterile, metallic,

they have met for the first time

chatted as elementary school classmates,

had so many questions for each other and so much

of their shared memory forgotten,

this is how it comes to everyone

who know all along that it is inevitable

who give to certainty what is due,

who do not preach about rebirthing snails,

who do not begin a sentence with exceptions,

and material certainties

who used to be sad-mouthed high school students,

who framed their days to indicate that time

we only make for each other,

out of vectors and shapes,

it comes to everyone like that
who never denied that they will meet,
who did not sigh at the world
who do not see Jesus on a toasted piece of bread,
and do not search for patterns in randomness,
who instead of self-delusionary lectures
and open letters
pair socks
this is how it comes
awkwardly, cheerfully,
languidly and indulgently,
blessed are the eternally disillusioned,
because death is theirs.

On Birdwings I Would Become Free
R.B. Bunn, Winston-Salem, NC

Sitting on the gray ground, I look up
The sky is a whirlpool of dark clouds
And lightning carving the sky into ruts
Yet I am stuck, to wonder aloud

What would it be like to grow wings
Glorious wings flushed with feathers
And alight to the realm where the wind sings
And leave the ground untethered

I could cross this troubled land
Littered with fields of dried stalks
Choaked by ashes so they no longer stand
And streams so thin that to call them river's, I'd balk

Is there something beyond where I am?
This place consumed by greedy fires
And tainted by ignorant hands
Where is this place that I desire?

I sit atop the sharp edge of a cliff
The drop feeds me hypnotizing lines
Falling is almost like flying, isn't it?
A question for trying times

It's a freedom of a kind is it not?
Icarus may have fallen
But he felt the sun before he dropped
Such thoughts they are calling

If only I was blessed with wings
I would fly so high to make a puddle of the sea
Freeing myself from tattered red strings
Knowing that, on birdwings, I would become free

Repeat: the narcissist effect
Allyssa Rose, Olean, NY

It's being left alone in a room I can't leave,
watching the annoying fly drain my mentality by seconds.
It's walking around a stranger every single step you take.
The bad coffee in the morning,
and late night waves of sadness
It's having to listen to the things that once intrigued me,
and swallowing the opinions that no longer matter.
A little bit leaves and never seems to return;
repeat.
It's actively trying to speak yet everything that comes out just isn't right.
It's tiptoeing around needles while avoiding the bombs
It's broken records playing through my eardrums
A fight or flight reaction;
fearing for my mind and letting it crumble at the same time;
repeat.
It's fire burning through my veins,
and a blush red face dripping sweat to my chin.
Its clenching my jaw filled with impulsiveness
and anger bursting out of my body.
Words not meant to be spoken
and punches not meant to be thrown.
Tears dripping from exhaustion;
repeat.
It's smiling at the smallest victory
watching it turn to ashes in my hands.
It's waking up a whole new person to be thrown back four steps by noon.
It's gazing around in my head from the little bit of attention received,

to watch it disintegrate in front of my eyes.

Butterflies filling my stomach embossed in anxiety and happiness

and yet, I grip to the least bit of elevation,

repeat.

Wanting out but not knowing how to unlock the door.

Wanting to scream my last goodbye but not knowing how to speak.

Wanting to cool the fire raging in my soul but not knowing where the water is.

Wanting the victory, but it's too far away,

so instead, I repeat.

Lighting a Candle
Clarence Poisson, Federal Way, WA

I came home from a jetty I frequent, where I looked
to sea horizon for a ship that left port with my man,
I didn't see any ships returning; I hope
my man is safe at sea in the artic fishing.
I'm always conscious of him at sea,
he lives a life of hazard from high seas,
strong winds and powerful storms. I don't
know if he'll come home; I know he has to do
this work and he's good doing it.

When I get home I light a candle for him,
I pray and invoke my ancestors to keep him safe.
I don't advertise my actions in faith,
most people won't believe such action anyway
but my faith is mostly for me to maintain my hope
that my man will come home.

I cannot prove prayer and invoking ancestors for protection works,
but when my man comes home, I'm justified.
There are those people who say, "Your actions in faith are nonsense."
They, cannot prove my faith in action is rubbish, of no foundation
and is pish-posh! Those people practice the same emotions
in and out of their scientific practices when they say,
"I hope this test works," or say, "I love you dear; I love you little one!"

But all emotions, out of science or in science
emanate from the same sources of the brain
and are intangible but can be acted upon.
My lighting a candle is an act of trust in what cannot be seen,
and an act of faith in prayer and invoking my ancestors,
for me; for my mental wellbeing, for hope
until I go to the jetty again and look to the horizon
for the ship that will return my man home from the sea.

Whole Soil Web
Patsy Asuncion, Charlottesville, VA

There is a necessary wisdom in the give-and-take of nature –
its quiet agreements and search for balance.
- Suzanne Simmard

Largest and oldest   Mother Trees   provide for the entire forest   the
wood wide web
seedlings   saplings   trees   fungi   bugs   creatures

below   at   above ground

Their teats of deep roots and fungi
   with love for all kindred
      quench thirst of shallow-rooted seedlings   subject to fickle weather
      feed   sugar   carbon   nitrogen   to hungry saplings
      reduce roots in high-traffic areas open up roads for flourishing families

   without prejudice to species
      share food with immigrant trees that speak different languages
      adapt neighborly help along seasonal shifts
         like Douglas Firs that   share cups of sugar with Birch in   spring
and fall
         and Birch that   return cups of sugar to Douglas Firs in summer

   with memory and intelligence in tree rings and seed DNA
      empower diverse species   to cooperatively resist   hotter and
drier conditions

despite the velocity of global warming   always ahead of wood-
land guardians
Climate change   calls   for survival of us all   not man's survival of the
fittest
  For survival of the whole soil web   Planet Earth
  Mankind   must cultivate the ways of Mother Trees

**with love for all kindred without prejudice to species with memory
and intelligence**

below   at   above ground

Chains of Patience
Sonia Elizabeth Teodorescu, Tampa, FL

I built 500 paper cranes waiting for you
and the wind was icy, and the sky was blue
and somewhere in a little garden
50 paper roses grew.

I built 500 paper cranes but
they couldn't fly because
I jacked their wings up, sort of.
So now they sit in a row on the window
sills, and on my dresser, and peeping past curtains.
They're looking out to the street and
watching people walk by.
As time passes them, they're stuck,
in soundless and still flight.

I built 500 paper cranes and thought
it would have a meaning (because everything always does)
between you and between me but
I might as well have never made them.
500 is not a big number when
infinity watches me with patient eyes.
I don't know if I should call it waiting,
when waiting doesn't feel like the right word.
There's bits of paper in the sky and in the Earth,
and maybe an artist could've drawn something of it,
and maybe a writer could've said something on it,
and maybe a mathematician could've seen something in it but,

there are 500 paper cranes,
around me and in my mind,
and gathering dust and running time,
and you still haven't come to say hi.

I built 500 paper cranes waiting for you and
not a single one of them could fly.

The Pileated
Carrie Cantalupo Sharp, Maple City, MI

his demented cry
announces his return
swooping wide winged
land in that maple tree
his red skull
immediately hatchets
where he'd left off yesterday

the cd's and tinsel I'd hung
ward him off
for a while

and now here he is
not to be fooled
his cry of hilarity
the joke is obviously on me

Shiva
Terry Chess, Wilmette, IL

Traditional seven-day period of mourning
observed by Jews after death of a loved one -

No one builds marble memorials to blue whales.
Or flies flags at half-staff for ape and elephant.
And most folks don't mourn Monarch butterflies

But this afternoon I found a dead mouse in my yard.
I'd heard faint squeaking by my window for days,
and dismissed it as a sound of the outdoor A/C unit.

It was brown.
The open eyes stared at me as I scooped its stiff body
up with a snow shovel, shrouded it in an old rag,
and tossed it in the trash. Suddenly I had this ludicrous thought:
who'll sit shiva?

The Power of One
Kasia Badger, Frisco, TX

In the heart of chaos, where shadows grow,
A single voice can rise, can roar,
A wave of courage, fierce and strong,
A call that echoes, "No more, no more."

Hands that once trembled, now clasp tight,
A circle forged in fire's light,
A bond that neither time nor fear,
Can break, can bend, can disappear.

We are the power of the sea,
Each drop a force, each drop a key,
To doors once locked by hate and lies,
Now thrown wide open to the skies.

When we unite, the earth will quake,
With every step that we dare take,
For in our numbers, strength is found,
A force that shakes the very ground.

No wall too high, no night too long,
Can stand against our unified song,
We are the hope that never dies,
The stars that light the darkest skies.

Together, we are more than dreams,
We are the river, we are the streams,
That carve through stone, that shape the land,
United hearts, united hands.

So let them come with all their might,
With all their greed, with all their spite,
For we will rise, and we will stand,
A world reborn, hand in hand.

This is our vow, this is our creed,
To stand as one in word and deed,
For in our unity, we find,
The strength to leave no soul behind.

Together, we are more than one,
Together, battles can be won,
We are the flame that never dies—
In unity, we reach the skies.

Coltrane
Beatriz Zimmermann, Bronx, NY

So, what does a white chick know about Coltrane?

I know how he makes me feel.
Buzzed and beautiful.
Young. But full of ancestral wisdom.

Impossibly free.
Swimming in the illusion that everything's fine.
When I know better.

Each note, all-knowing.

I climb on and ride, never wanting to get off.
Soaking up the divine.

The things we think but never say just wash away.
The things we need and never find, hardly matter.

I suddenly have just enough.
Eternity in every note.

When One Life Feels Enough
Anoushka Majumder, San Diego, CA

"Doubled-over laughing / on wet grass, a smile / too wide, too / bright
to be / real, a joy / too immense, too / heavy, too / liberating for a
single / soul.

An overlapping rhythm of slowing / heartbeats and clocks, an /
overpowering urge to fall / over, into an / abyss, a meadow in / full
bloom, or this star-studded / galaxy. An / overdue exhale ridden with
hopes too / sweet to taste, too distant to / see.

Eyes outlined by bittersweet / tears falling like / feathers, butterflies, /
blissfully unaware of / air, resistance, until / the beautiful becomes
painfully / bitter and breath / turns to / stone.

Broken glass from the / sun, a patchwork quilt of / feelings pieced
together with a thread called / fear, a girl / running against the / rain,
gravity, time, the warping of a world burning, brimming / with life.
Stargazing on a frigid evening in / November, and one, just / one,
moment of forgotten, unadulterated / silence."

"And that," she / whispered, under her / breath, "is the story / of my
life in one memory, one / song."

To the Quiet Knoll
Lee Orlich Bertram, Moscow, ID

Muted thoughts telepathed between us,
as we cast down bleary eyes in respect,
encumbered by a reserve scored by years of footfalls
echoing on the worn tiled floors of our history.

Transcendence—no expression of actual words,
for we could vividly envision
from private years past, the collection
of heavy tears on the tips of mascaraed lashes.

Mired down in unthinkable sorrow,
sounds of a country bleeding, trickling
off and pooling onto the sheet music below,
tear by solitary tear.

Creating a stain for all mankind, compromising
our joy in childhood, a song of mortality and eternal rest.
We hesitated for an instant as we climbed,
a channeling zephyr grazed our aged faces.

Mourning all over again the happening when our
lives were forever suspended in a void.
A waft of lavender roses snuggled
in our unsteady hands,
waiting to whither near the eternal flame,
a tribute to the man once beloved by the world.

We performed the music obediently in December,
flashes of notes ricocheted off the walls of recounting,
turning and glancing over one shoulder,
to hear the phantom piano not there.

In Paradisum sounded but for an instant,
then bore him safely away from relentless tragedy.

In Paradisum,
Deducant te Angeli.

Hurry
Annya Broderick, Wilmington, NC

I don't want to hurry.

I don't want to move so fast that
I don't hear the sounds of my own footsteps,
or the wings of the honeybees dancing with the Queen Anne's lace,
or the soft, blue wake of a dark-hulled boat a 'sea.

I don't want to rush through my life
and miss seeing the horses running down the downs,
or the shiny crows singin' a 'top a fence post,
or the bend of the earth as it meets the sky rendering the horizon useless.

I don't want to miss my life.
I have been away for fifty-three days now.
When we focus too intensely on getting somewhere,
we miss everything.

People keep asking,
Where are you going?
What are you doing?
I don't know,
I don't know.

I don't care to be busy.

As I drive my legs up and down these Seven Sisters,
my mind wanders and writes stories as it often does...

Once upon a time,
I wandered these fields in only my fresh white petticoat,
because it was midsummer and the animals don't mind my not being proper.

Once upon a time, I rode my horse to the edge of the land,
and stared at the sea for hours on end,
then picked wildflowers and tended to my sheeps and cats.

Once upon a time, I wrote love letters with quill and ink,
I wrote poems and stories of the glittering trails of wandering snails,
I wrote in late summer afternoons, until I lost my mind, until I lost the light.

My mind has grown spacious and quiet,
I've surrendered into the undoing.

I don't want to move so fast through life that life doesn't touch me.

Millennium Jubilee
Deborah DeNicola, Margate, FL

We were called to attend the fake alien invasion. The subpoena arrived in a blue vellum envelope with a stamp of clouds and empty sky and a watermark hologram of a dove. They gave the date and time but Jim noticed the venue was missing. He said it was because we might be portal jumping and did not know the cyber space where we 'd end up. I wanted to go as a cosmic diamond so as to flood the ballroom with my light. Amy asked if the occasion was a pre-requisite to the Fake Jesus Resurrection we'd prayed against—but we all agreed that would only come later on, like after we slid our bodies into our alien outfits. I decided my auric field would be fuchsia with a tint of lavender or peach. Sandy was conjuring her acoustic vortex to slide right on down the sound of Tibetan bells into the stardust skin-suit the tones produced. The day of— we costumed up early, went all theta-like under the dancing frequency of the singing bowls I'd psycho-neurally sensed and orbs of change everywhere in the air, trees vibrating and grass waving it's sheafs like clapping hands. I expected to see Whitman and Neruda. Or at least Rimbaud in his drunken boat and Wacko Jacko moon-walking-on-water. If they could fake aliens, why not singers, dancers and poets? And wouldn't that be the change we wanted to see in the world? After all, I'd practiced handwriting in raindrops ever since I was young, poems like drones buzzing my dreamscape. We knew we could metabolize the higher vibes but wanted more than to live in a simulation. Nonetheless, to our surprise a ship arrived on time and Jim said something new was coming—or going—while I felt in my clipped wings something huge about to bubble up.

All I know about love
Sarah Oguntomilade, Charlotte, NC

Do not worry so much about when love will arrive.
In the same way that you shouldn't worry about when the wind will blow
or when the tide will rise.
Love is an inevitable force of nature.

Do not worry so much about where love is when it is not with you.
In the same way that you shouldn't worry about where the cows do in
the winter
or where the moon hides when it does not shine in the night sky.
Love is no minder of man.

Do not worry about how long love will stay.
In the same way that you shouldn't worry about how long your shadow
will trail behind you
or for how long the river Nile will flow through Egypt.
Love is a constant shapeshifter.

The truth of the matter is you can run away all you want.
But one day someone is going to take a hold of you
And love you
And maybe touch you
And who knows? Maybe they'll even stick around

Then you'll have no choice but to look in the mirror
And prove yourself wrong about being unlovable.

At Washelli Memorial Gardens (for mother)
Norman Goodwin, Seattle, WA

Above, the pale spring sky is scuffed with cloud,
a purple smear that's soon pastelled by wind,
while all around, in warming air, the bowed
and flowered limbs of cherries, plums, rescind
the claims of winter's clench, ensure return
of what last fall had darkened, fallen, spoiled.
Mid-April's flared the colors back. They burn
and shine like rainbowed hues on slicks of oil.

Below, an inscribed stone to mark an urn
commemorates another April date,
reminding me to grasp what won't return.
That loss, by measure weightless, carries weight.
I visit here on warmer days each spring.
The loss is lessoned by the blossoming.

The Cleveland Hills
Jenny Doughty, Portland, ME

Who should know eternity better than hills
that live in geologic time? North Yorkshire hills
have stored secrets and sea creatures since the Jurassic.

Between them young green dales and cowslip meadows
run where great ice sheets groaned and ground,
and dry-stone walls enclose more sheep than people.

The hills watch stone circles, castles and abbeys rise
then ruin. Walk across the moors from Helmsley to Rievaulx
on causeways built by Romans and see stones tumbled away,

remains of Gothic arches like decayed teeth.
An iron wind rushes over treeless scarps,
through crooked thorn bushes bent to its will,

over purple heather scrub, the rippled skin
of crab grass, and buffets stoic sheep that wait
for feed while the slaughter truck chugs along the road.

In a gnat-bite of time I picnicked on the moors
by a packhorse bridge over a peat-brown stream.
Father lit the primus stove to boil water for tea,

mother spread a picnic cloth while I searched in the beck
for fossils then lay back in the heather under clear sky
and lark song as if I were growing out of the earth.

Omar

Jerry Smaldone, Arvada, CO

I heard him walk across the floor above me
Creaking in that same spot, to his cooler
Take something out, cheese, hard cheese

And walk away, crutch thumping
Stop suddenly,
Walk back and grab a cold soda

The accordion was playing lightly in the background
Blurred by the walls, while he talked and talked
Sang a little and told his compadres

How he wished he could have gone home
For the funeral, but in the end, it was just too far,
There was too much work, too many commitments

How his cousin would miss him, how she loved
Her son-in-law, only 32, his wet eyes shining
When he said it would be good to be there, you know

For her, and then thought of how good it would feel
To be back in that dusty little own outside Juarez
A return to the comfort of the familiar

And then it poured out, the leukemia, how they'd
Given him five weeks to live, his two year old
daughter, don't let me leave her dear god, not yet,

and here he was, alive and kicking, with his broken leg,
life is too short I heard him say, as he climbed the ladder,
stroked more paint and sang, one song about death,

one song about life.

THE DIVE
Marilyn Brodhurst, Tucson, AZ

I visit my friend
     S T R E T C H E D
     to capacity...
Her six month's prognosis
Into a twelve-year battle.

We share our lunch
     S U B M E R G E D
In rippling laughter.

Her wit conjures magic
Wrought by a discarded
past.
     A N O I N T E D
By struggles with
Discordant partners,
We torched our way into
Feminine independence.

     S C R U B B E D
Now by spirals of
Incensed-prayer
We are
     F R E E D
From illusions
Of who we were.

Quietly I watch her,
       PULSED
By staccato breath.
       POISED…
Knowing soon
She will
       PLUNGE
                    Leaving me…

       SWIMMING
Into swirls
Of light.

I'm Sorry I Can't Be a Coffee Coaster
Amelie Peterson, Trinidad, CA

I wish I could say I didn't know from experience
That the boundary I tediously drew
Is the only thing keeping you here

I know you think that you're different from the rest
I'm sorry that makes you just like the rest

I'm only worth earning, only worth having
As long as I'm just out of reach

You only want to know more
As long as something is kept a secret

You only value my vulnerability
If I'm never completely vulnerable

You only want meif you think there's a chance
That if you gave it your best shot, you couldn't earn me

A jigsaw puzzle incomplete is a challenge
A jigsaw puzzle solved is a coaster for a coffee cup
Or maybe just atable ornament

I'm only exciting if I'm not excited
I'm only captivating if I'm not captivated

You'll want to look at me all day
As long as you know that you can look away
Before I catch you looking

I'm sorry that you're not the first, second or third
To hold me only long enough for a selfie
To care for me only as long as I fit on a bracelet or in a pocket

I'm incapable of allowing myself to be a coaster one more time.
I'll take my chances with going unsolved

ONE PAGE POETRY

Made in the USA
Las Vegas, NV
14 December 2024